WINSLOW HOMER

Winslow Homer

by MARY A. JUDGE

CROWN PUBLISHERS, INC. - NEW YORK

Title page: WINSLOW HOMER AT PROUT'S NECK
Unknown Photographer, 1908
Bowdoin College Museum of Art, Brunswick, Maine
Gift of the Homer family

Series published under the direction of:
MADELEINE LEDIVELEC-GLOECKNER

Editorial research and layout:
MARIE-HÉLÈNE AGÜEROS

Library of Congress Cataloging in Publication Data

Judge, Mary.
    Winslow Homer.

    (The Q.L.P. art series)
    1. Homer, Winslow, 1836-1910.   I. Title.
N6537.H58A4   1986   759.13   86-2615
ISBN O-517-55725-8

PRINTED IN ITALY – INDUSTRIE GRAFICHE CATTANEO S.P.A., BERGAMO
© 1986 BONFINI PRESS CORPORATION, NAEFELS, SWITZERLAND

PRISONERS FROM THE FRONT, 1866
Oil on canvas, 24″ × 38″ (61 × 96.5 cm)
The Metropolitan Museum of Art, New York. Gift of Mrs. Frank B. Porter

Winslow Homer's professional career began just before the outbreak of the Civil War and ended with his death in 1910, four years before the First World War. In the course of this time, America developed from a primarily agricultural nation to the world's leading industrial power. Culturally, however, this country still looked to Europe for a bona fide artistic tradition and for artistic training. Homer visited Europe twice, stayed briefly, and returned to go about his «business of art» independently, eventually on a remote part of the Maine coast. He had found what he wanted to paint and he set about doing it with as little interference from the outside world as possible. He was the quintessential New England Yankee—self-reliant, strong-willed, practical, terse—whose approach to art was much the same. He worked from physical, observable fact, whether on East Coast farmlands and seashores, in his early years, or on the rugged Maine coast, the Adirondack and Quebec wilderness, or the tropics, in his maturity. Much like the realist Gustave Courbet, he

Wounded Soldier Being Given a Drink from a Canteen, 1864
Charcoal and white chalk on green paper
$14^3/_8$" × $19^{15}/_{16}$" (36.5 × 50 cm)
Cooper-Hewitt Museum, The Smithsonian Institution's
National Museum of Design, New York

insisted on painting unembellished ordinary life, with a thickly applied brush that affirmed the materiality of forms and substances. He painted out of doors in the Barbizon tradition, often finishing his work in the studio, and shared with many of his French contemporaries, among them Edouard Manet, an interest in Oriental principles of design. (A speck of red, common in Japanese prints, is visible in many of his paintings). Although he was concerned with the effect of light and atmosphere on matter, his forms were arranged in sharp patterns and silhouettes, retaining their spatial separateness, instead of dissipating into impressionistic specks of color and light. These artistic preoccupations were common to many painters internationally and were not necessarily a matter of particular direct influencing.

In Homer's early years, his American counterparts worked mostly in genre subjects or in landscape. Homer himself had begun his career as an illustrator, and his work in this medium shows a strong sense of design, which he retained throughout his career, and a storytelling element that later became more mythic than narrative. His early paintings, often of similar subjects as the engravings, grew out of the genre tradition. Had he stopped working in the 1870s, he would have been remembered as a good painter of nineteenth-century life. It was not until he turned seriously to man's relationship to nature and to nature as a subject itself that he achieved the artistic magnitude for which he is remembered today. In keeping with the transcendental philosophies of Ralph Waldo Emerson and Henry David Thoreau, landscape painting up until midcentury had expressed nature as a source for reverence, as something for man's contemplation: To Homer, nature was a challenge, something to be studied and respected; something that had little use for man.

Homer made his monumental statements in oils, rearranging forms from life to express an elemental power and simplicity that was drawn from common experience and perceived in tonalities of light against dark. In his watercolors he was freer, using vibrant, unlikely

Young Soldier (Separate
Study of a Soldier Giving
Water to a Wounded
Companion), 1861
Oil, gouache and graphite
14 $^3/_{16}$″ × 7 $^3/_{16}$″ (36 × 18.2 cm)
Cooper-Hewitt Museum
The Smithsonian Institution's
National Museum of Design
New York
Gift of Charles Savage Homer

The Army of the Potomac — A Sharpshooter on Picket Duty, 1862
Wood engraving on paper, 9¹/₈″ × 13¹³/₁₆″ (23.2 × 35 cm)
National Museum of American Art, Smithsonian Institution, Washington, D.C.
Gift of the International Business Machine Corporation

colors side by side in a looser hand. The work was fresher, more immediate and intimate than his oils and had little artistic heritage from which to build. Homer felt his greatest contribution was in this medium.

Homer was a nineteenth-century man who chose to ignore the material progress of the century and concentrate on the rustic life, remnants from his youth, representing a man's world of hunting, fishing, and outdoor work. His early work revealed the Victorian manners of propriety and a strain between the sexes, a world in which even eye contact was rarely achieved. In his later paintings the sexes were segregated until the figurative element all but disappeared. Yet his mature work was very modern, barely representational. It verged on abstraction and in its deceptive simplicity achieved a sense of inexplicable mystery.

There is scant documentation of Homer's life and thoughts. When approached by his future biographer, William H. Downes, concerning the proposed book, Homer replied,

8

It may seem ungrateful to you that after your twenty-five years of hard work booming my pictures I should not agree with you in regard to that proposed sketch of my life. But I think that it would probably kill me to have such [a] thing appear, and as the most interesting part of my life is of no concern to the public, I must decline to give you any particulars in regard to it.[1]

As a result, we must rely on Homer's letters to his family and to his dealers, the accounts and reminiscences of some of his contemporaries, and, above all, on the work itself.

Early nineteenth-century Boston was at the heart of Yankee America—a mercantile, seafaring city with a cultural tradition more advanced in literature than in art; a city where the public art gallery was established in a wing of the library. Winslow Homer was born in the harbor district at 25 Friend Street on February 24, 1836, the second of three sons, to Charles Savage and Henrietta Maria Benson Homer. Both parents were of solid New England stock, from respectable if not prosperous middle-class families. His father was an importer of hardware; his mother, originally from Maine, a watercolor painter.

(1) Winslow Homer to William H. Downes, letter of August 1908. Quoted in William H. Downes, *The Life and Works of Winslow Homer*. Boston: Houghton, Mifflin, 1911, p. 234.

Three Days on the Front, ca 1863
Black chalk on blue paper, 8 15/16" × 17 3/4" (22.8 × 45.1 cm)
Cooper-Hewitt Museum
The Smithsonian Institution's National Museum of Design, New York

Our National Winter Exercise—Skating
Wood engraving, 20½" × 14" (52 × 35.5 cm)
Frank Leslie's Illustrated Newspaper, January 13, 1866, pp. 264-265
The Library of Congress, Washington, D.C.

When Homer was six, the family moved to the more rural Cambridge, where his mother had been raised, and finally settled on Garden Street across from the Common, near Harvard University. Cambridge provided ideal surroundings for a boy growing up, with its fields, forests, and streams nearby, so much so that fishing and the outdoor life remained lifelong loves and subjects for his work. Never much of a student, at an early age Homer showed an interest in drawing that was encouraged by his parents. His mother was a serious artist, probably she gave him some instruction. His father sent him sketchbooks and lithographs to copy and study from his frequent travels abroad. One of Homer's childhood drawings, *Adolescence* (Bowdoin College), shows a boy lying in the grass daydreaming, not unlike his later oil painting and engraving *The Nooning* (ca 1872, Wadsworth Atheneum). His happy associations with childhood are apparent in the work of his early years.

When Winslow was thirteen, his father sold the family business, invested in mining machinery, and took off for California in an ill-fated scheme to strike it rich in the Gold Rush. Young

Winslow drew a cartoon of his father crossing the Rockies on a rocket to commemorate the event—and forty years later he was still drawing satirical cartoons of his father. With diminished family funds and an unremarkable scholastic record, Homer's prospects for college were dismal at best. While reading the newspaper one morning, his father spotted a help-wanted ad for «a boy with a taste for drawing: no other wanted,»[1] and encouraged him to try for the position. As it happened, the owner of the printmaking firm, John H. Bufford, was a volunteer fireman along with the senior Homer. And so, at the age of nineteen, Homer was apprenticed as a lithographer for a two-year term. This was to be his first artistic training.

For approximately the next thirty years, Homer experimented with a variety of media (engravings, watercolors, oil paintings), subjects (soldiers, women, children, blacks), and

(1) Quoted in Lloyd Goodrich, *Winslow Homer.* New York: Whitney Museum of American Art and Macmillan, 1944, p. 5.

A Parisian Ball—Dancing at the Casino
Wood engraving, 13¾″ × 5⅞″ (35 × 14.9 cm)
Harper's Weekly, November 23, 1867, p. 745
The Library of Congress, Washington, D.C.

locales (Boston, New York City, Gloucester, the Adirondacks, Virginia). But it was not until he returned from England in the early 1880s that he really began to find his own voice. Up until this point his work was accomplished and well recognized by his peers, but it was not truly distinctive, not yet of the distinguished stature he achieved with his great paintings of the 1890s onwards.

EARLY WORKS

Homer's earliest assignments for Bufford's were to design the covers for sheet music of popular songs, such as « The Ratcatcher's Daughter, » « Katy Darling, » and « Oh Whistle and I'll Come to You, My Lad. » His talent was recognized quickly and soon he advanced to preparing a print consisting of forty-two individual portraits of the entire Massachusetts Senate, probably taken from photographs. While at Bufford's he met future painters Joseph E. Baker and Joseph Foxcroft Cole. It was to Cole that he later remarked, « If a man wants to be an artist, he should never look at pictures. »[1]

(1) Quoted in Lloyd Goodrich, *ibid.*, p. 6.

◁
Husking the Corn in New England
Wood engraving
13⅞″ × 9¼″ (35.3 × 23.5 cm)
Harper's Weekly, November 13, 1858, p. 728
The Library of Congress, Washington, D.C.

THE MORNING BELL, ca 1866
Oil on canvas, 24″ × 38¼″ (36.7 × 97.2 cm)
Yale University Art Gallery
New Haven, Connecticut
Bequest of Stephen Carlton Clark

THE CROQUET MATCH, 1868-1869
Oil on board, 9¾″ × 15½″ (24.7 × 39.4 cm)
Private collection

LONG BRANCH, NEW JERSEY, 1869
Oil on canvas, 16″ × 21¾″ (40.6 × 55.2 cm)
Museum of Fine Arts, Boston
Charles Henry Hayden Fund

THE CROQUET PLAYERS, 1865
Oil on canvas, 16″ × 26″ (40.7 × 66 cm)
Albright-Knox Art Gallery, Buffalo, New York
Charles Clifton and James G. Forsyth Funds

Despite better assignments and the reduction of most of his three-hundred-dollar apprentice fee, Homer left Bufford's as soon as his term was up, rented a studio in the Ballou Publishing building in Boston, and began his career as an independent illustrator at the age of twenty-one. While there he met the French engraver Damoreau, who introduced him to the technique of wood engraving, a simpler, less time-consuming process than etching. Wood engravings were then being used to illustrate pictorial weeklies, a new form of periodical in America. Homer's early works, published in «Ballou's Pictorial Drawing Room Companion» and the recently founded «Harper's Weekly» in New York, depict everyday city life—street scenes, anecdotal scenes of men and women—and homespun country life. The lively *Husking the Corn in New England* illustrated a local tradition: When a young man finds an ear of red corn, he is entitled to a kiss from the nearest young lady (see page 12).

Waverly Oaks, 1875-1878
Graphite, white gouache on gray-green paper
5¹³/₁₆" × 8¹/₁₆" (14.8 × 20.4 cm)
Cooper-Hewitt Museum, The Smithsonian Institution's National Museum of Design, New York
Gift of Charles Savage Homer

By the fall of 1859, it looked as if Ballou's was about to fold. Homer decided to move to New York, where there was greater opportunity for a young artist. He was offered a permanent position at «Harper's,» but adamantly declined: «I had had a taste of freedom. The slavery of Bufford's was too fresh in my recollection to let me care to bind myself again. From the time that I took my nose off that lithographer's stone, I have had no master, and never shall have any.»[1]

He first took a room in a boardinghouse on East Sixteenth Street, and briefly attended a drawing school in Brooklyn. He entered night school at the National Academy of Design on Thirteenth Street, but did not like the constrictive academic approach, and quickly left. Otherwise, his only known formal instruction consisted of a few lessons with the now little-known genre and landscape painter Frédéric Rondel. By 1861, he had moved into the New York

(1) Winslow Homer to George W. Sheldon. Quoted in Lloyd Goodrich, *op. cit.*, p. 11.

"ALL IN THE GAY AND GOLDEN WEATHER."

ALL in the gay and golden weather,
Two fair travellers, maid and man,
Sailed in a birchen boat together,

And sailed the way that the river ran:
The sun was low, not set, and the west
Was colored like a robin's breast.

All in the Gay and Golden Weather
Wood engraving, 6½" × 5½" (16.5 × 14 cm)
Appleton's Journal of Literature, Science and Art
June 12, 1869, p. 312
The Library of Congress, Washington, D.C.

University Building on Washington Square, also occupied by painter Eastman Johnson. His studio was near the top of this Gothic-style building, approachable by a small stairway, and was described by one visitor as « altogether too small for a man to have a large idea in. » [1]

With the outbreak of the Civil War in 1861, Homer was sent in October to the Virginia front with the Army of the Potomac on assignment as an artist-correspondent for « Harper's Weekly, » and returned six months later to cover the Peninsular Campaign. Most of his illustrations from this period were completed back in New York from on-the-scene drawings. Reportorial and sometimes anecdotal, these works show the daily life of the soldier in its least romantic aspects—the endless hours of waiting in camp, the unceremonious meals, the sleeping on the battlefield. His few battle scenes—*The War for the Union, 1862*; *A Cavalry Charge* and *A Bayonet Charge* [2]— describe with uncharacteristic intensity unheroic, ferocious, hand-to-hand combat as experienced by a firsthand observer. The reality of this war was made increasingly visible to the populace at large through the publication of photographs taken under the aegis of Mathew Brady. Homer's work, particularly his paintings, shows an awareness of this new medium in his treatment of light and shadow, depth of field, and framing of a scene.

In *Bivouac Fire on the Potomac*, a pervasive tension underlies a seemingly relaxing moment in wartime (see page 30). The huge shadow of the sentinel's head looms against the background tent while the fire brightens the steely tip of his bayonet. The few silhouetted figures in the front are flattened into design patterns, a technique common in Japanese prints

(1) Thomas Bailey Aldrich, quoted in James Thomas Flexner, *The World of Winslow Homer, 1836-1910*. New York: Time Incorporated, 1966, p. 35.
(2) *Harper's Week*, July 5, 1862, pp. 424-425 and July 12, 1862, pp. 440-441.

and adopted by the French artist Edouard Manet. Similarly, *The Army of the Potomac —
A Sharpshooter on Picket Duty*, based on an oil painting of the same title, shows an affinity
to Japanese design in its asymmetrical placement of the figure (see page 8). More poignant
is the oil study of a *Young Soldier*, a portrait of a vulnerable boy dressed for a man's job
(see page 7).

According to his friend Roswell Morse Shurtleff, Homer's first completed oil painting was
Sharpshooter, which he decided to sell for «not less than sixty dollars, as that was what
"Harper's" paid him for a full page drawing on wood.»[1] Intent on making a living from
his art, he put it up for exhibition along with a painting of a soldier punished for intoxication,
and threatened to accept the full-time job at «Harper's» if they did not sell. Fortunately,
they did. It was not until years later, however, that he learned that the purchaser had been

(1) William H. Downes, *op. cit.*, p. 47.

The Beach at Long Branch
Wood engraving, 19⅜" × 13" (49.2 × 33 cm)
Appleton's Journal of Literature, Science and Art, August 21, 1869
The Metropolitan Museum of Art, New York. Harris Brisbane Dick Fund

THE BERRY PICKERS, 1873
Watercolor on paper
9⅜" × 13⅝" (23.8 × 34.7 cm)
Museum of Art, Colby College
Waterville, Maine

▷
Snap-The-Whip
Wood engraving
12¾" × 8⅜" (32.4 × 21.3 cm)
Harper's Weekly
September 20, 1873, pp. 824-825
The Metropolitan Museum of Art, New York
Harris Brisbane Dick Fund

his brother Charles. Nevertheless, Homer's oils found buyers outside his family and received a favorable press: «These works are real; the artist paints what he has seen and known.»[1] Such a comment appropriately describes his entire œuvre.

In 1864, Homer was elected an associate of the National Academy of Design, and in the following year was elected a member at the young age of twenty-nine. *Prisoners from the Front*, completed after the war, was shown at the Academy in 1866 (see page 5). The painting established his reputation. It shows a confrontation between members of the opposing sides, a Union officer and three Confederate prisoners, in the aftermath of battle. With a reporter's skill, Homer refines the composition to its essentials: He individualizes each man's expression and pose, grouped the ragtag Confederates in a frieze and separated them from the commanding officer with a pronounced spatial gap. Behind the officer are his troops; surrounding the prisoners is a ravaged, desolate landscape, with their surrendered rifles in front. It is uncertain whether this painting was based on an actual event or was a composite of fact and fiction.[2] Although Homer painted from life, he often altered his

(1) *London Art Journal*, quoted in James Thomas Flexner, *op. cit.*, p. 69.
(2) See Nicolai Cikovsky, Jr., «Winslow Homer's Prisoners from the Front,» *Metropolitan Museum Journal*, 12 (1977), p. 172.

The Robin's Note
Wood engraving, 9" × 8⅞" (22.8 × 22.6 cm)
Every Saturday, August 20, 1870, frontispiece
The Library of Congress, Washington, D.C.

compositions to suit his purposes. The Union officer may be Brigadier-General Francis Channing Barlow.[1] Barlow, who had been a college classmate of Homer's brother Charles, had assisted Homer during his visit to the front in April 1862. According to Barlow's son, Homer posed the more fit General Miles for the body and placed Barlow's head on top. Later annoyed at the continuing popularity of this painting to the neglect of his more mature works, Homer exclaimed, « I'm sick of hearing about that picture. »[2]

In the fall of 1866, Homer left New York for a yearlong stay in Paris, his first trip abroad. He shared a studio on Montmartre with fellow artist Albert Warren Kelsey, and occasionally enjoyed Paris night life, as is evident in the dance-hall scenes of *A Parisian Ball — Dancing at the Mabille, Paris*[3] and *A Parisian Ball — Dancing at the Casino* (see page 11), subjects later painted by Henri de Toulouse-Lautrec. He visited the Louvre, where he drew the student copyists for an engraving, and must have seen the Universal Exposition of 1867, where *Prisoners from the Front* was on display. Outside the fairgrounds, Gustave Courbet and Edouard Manet mounted an independent show of their controversial paintings to protest their exclusion from the main event. Although we have no written record of Homer's activities in France, it is likely that he saw their work. He shared Courbet's realist approach and his handling of paint and Manet's insistence on contemporary subject matter and his spatial arrangement of simplified and flattened forms that massed into areas of lights and darks, inspired by the Japanese prints that circulated in Paris at the time. Whether these

(1) Nicolai Cikovsky, Jr., first proposed the connection between Brigadier-General Barlow and Homer, *op. cit.*, pp. 155-172. Natalie Spassky explained Barlow's association with the Homer family and provided an account of Homer's portrait of Barlow, quoted from Barlow's son. Natalie Spassky, *Winslow Homer at the Metropolitan Museum of Art.* New York: Metropolitan Museum of Art, 1982, p. 11.
(2) Quoted in Lloyd Goodrich, *op. cit.*, p. 51.
(3) *Harper's Weekly*, November 23, 1867, p. 744.

SUNLIGHT AND SHADOW, 1872
Oil on canvas, $15^{13}/_{16}'' \times 22^{3}/_{8}''$ (40.2 × 57.5 cm)
Cooper-Hewitt Museum, The Smithsonian
Institution's National Museum of Design, New York

GATHERING AUTUMN LEAVES, 1877
Oil on canvas
38³/₁₆″ × 24³/₈″ (97 × 61.8 cm)
Cooper-Hewitt Museum, The Smithsonian
Institution's National
Museum of Design, New York

THE TWO GUIDES, 1875 (?)
Oil on canvas
24¹/₄″ × 38¹/₄″ (61.3 × 97.1 cm)
The Sterling and Francine Clark Institute
Williamstown, Massachusetts

The Cotton Pickers, 1876
Oil on canvas, $24^{1}/_{16}$" × $38^{1}/_{8}$" (61.2 × 96.8 cm)
The Los Angeles County Museum of Art
Acquisition made possible through museum trustees

artists actually influenced Homer's work is debatable; evidence of these techniques was apparent in his work before he left for Paris. Japanese prints had already become available in the United States with the publication of Hiroshige's work accompanying the U. S. Government Report on Commodore Perry's expedition to Japan in 1856. And Homer might have come upon similar handling of forms in space through his years of experience as a printmaker. The first famous Impressionist exhibition did not occur for another seven years; and the work of Claude Monet at this time, for example, did not look fully impressionistic. Nevertheless, the concerns of these painters—explorations in light, color, and atmosphere were already apparent—concerns that were made manifest in America as well. Homer owned the Impressionist handbook, Michel-Eugène Chevreul's «The Laws of Contrast of Color,» as early as 1858. His approach differed from the French, however, in its emphasis on the definition of matter, of distinct objects in light, rather than on the description of light itself.

While many of Homer's Luminist contemporaries such as John F. Kensett and Martin J. Heade, studied American light through contemplative landscapes, Homer's use of light and landscape was integral to the study of figures in space. From the mid-1860s through the '70s, scenes from daily life predominate—life out of doors in the city, its environs, and the countryside. Like his French counterparts, he concentrated on the leisure activities of the middle class, and in the 1870s he particularly focused on attractive women (engaged in sport, as in the *Bridle Path* [Sterling and Francine Clark Institute], or at rest, as in *Sunlight and Shadow*; see page 25) and on children. His croquet series from 1865 to 1869, comprising five oil paintings, drawings, and wood engravings, demonstrate contemporary manners through the game itself and the interrelationships of the men and women who played it. Croquet was one example of a new freedom afforded women to engage in recreational activity with men, and became a metaphor for sexual relations, which, according to Homer, were frequently strained.[1] In *The Croquet Players* (1865), a trio of women punctuated by a tree dominate the foreground, in a composition comparable to Monet's 1866 *Women in the Garden* (see page 16). But whereas Monet's women revolve around the tree in the shimmering light of a pleasant afternoon, Homer's women seem as static as figurines, set in a murky late-day light, where shadows project in hardened patterns. The modulated color more resembles the palette of Manet. As in *Prisoners from the Front*, Homer used a spatial gap to separate the figure groups. Here a solitary man in a top hat is estranged from the women by a chasmic space between them, a visualization of frustration. Similarly in *Croquet Scene* (1866, Art Institute of Chicago), a central male is flanked by women on either side, seemingly locked into place. The top-hatted man turns up again in *Our National Winter Exercise— Skating* (see page 10), where he is singled out by his directly frontal position. The women's flattened belled dresses, billowing ribbons and hat veils create decorative patterns that occur in other formations in later work. The splayed figure adds an anecdotal but unsettling note

(1) See David Park Curry, *Winslow Homer: The Croquet Game*. New Haven, Conn.: Yale University Art Gallery, 1984.

to this seemingly charming scene. The same top-hatted man appears a third time in one of Homer's many beach engravings, *The Beach at Long Branch* (see page 19), where he is isolated and out of touch with the goings-on. Although Homer frequently used the same model for a number of works, it is possible that this figure was particularly significant.

The Croquet Match (see page page 14) marks a change in light quality—incidentally following his trip to France—that is shared by *Long Branch, New Jersey* (see page 15). In the former painting Homer sets up a system of weights and balances through color and placement building compositional structure. A group of figures at the tip of the abruptly asymmetrical porch contrasts with the lone figure on the lawn; the vertical white column held like a ship's mast counterbalances the standing figure in white in a posture of wistful anticipation, typical of nineteenth-century paintings. Like Japanese printmakers, Homer accented the scene with red; these characteristic touches appear throughout his work. In the Monet-like *Long Branch, New Jersey*, a woman is perched at the edge of the bluffs in a similar stance to that of the woman in white in *The Croquet Match*, but here the wistful expression is replaced by haughty

◁

A Bivouac Fire on the Potomac
Wood engraving
20¼" × 13¾" (51.4 × 35 cm)
Harper's Weekly, December 21, 1861
pp. 808-809
The Library of Congress, Washington, D.C.

THE CARNIVAL, 1877
Oil on canvas
20" × 30" (50.8 × 76.2 cm)
The Metropolitan Museum of Art
New York
Amelia S. Lazarus Fund

self-possession. These brighter, less photographic works were not necessarily well received. One critic wrote: «The success which attended *Prisoners from the Front* seems to have spoiled a good artist.»[1]

Although Homer lived in New York City for close to twenty years, he never painted an urban scene and, with a few early exceptions, rarely illustrated one in an engraving. During the late 1860s and the '70s, he would leave his New York studio to spend the spring and summer in New England, visiting his parents in Cambridge and then traveling to the seashore or to the mountains and farmlands of upstate New York. For the most part he chose to avoid representing industrialized America; he showed cityfolk in parks or at summer resorts, or countryfolk on the farm or in the rustic surroundings of his boyhood. In a rare look at a changing rural America, *The Morning Bell* shows a factory worker on her way to the mill. Cast in the harsh overhead light of early morning, she traverses the walkway as a prisoner on a gangplank (see page 13). The composition, literally built with structures, is patterned with a sensibility akin to prints of Japanese figures on bridges. But here the downward turn of the woman's hat and the droopy dog set a forlorn tone, while the vacant space

(1) Quoted from a Brooklyn newspaper in Lloyd Goodrich, *op. cit.*, p. 51.

Gloucester Harbor
Wood engraving, black ink on newsprint paper
11″ × 15¾″ (27.9 × 40 cm)
Harper's Weekly, September 27, 1872, p. 844
Cooper-Hewitt Museum
The Smithsonian Institution's National
Museum of Design, New York
Gift of Charles Savage Homer

BREEZING UP (A FAIR WIND), 1876
Oil on canvas
24⅛″ × 38⅛″ (61.5 × 97 cm)
National Gallery of Art, Washington, D.C.
Gift of the W. L. and
May T. Mellon Foundation

INSIDE THE BAR, TYNEMOUTH, 1883
Watercolor on paper, 15⅜″ × 28½″ (39 × 72.5 cm)
The Metropolitan Museum of Art, New York
Gift of Louise Ryals Arkell

BLOWN AWAY, ca 1888
Watercolor over pencil, $10^{1}/_{8}'' \times 19^{1}/_{16}''$ (25.5 × 48.4 cm)
The Brooklyn Museum, New York

GLASS WINDOWS, BAHAMAS, ca 1885
Watercolor over pencil, $13^{15}/_{16}'' \times 20^{1}/_{16}''$ (35.4 × 51 cm)
The Brooklyn Museum, New York

between them (as in *The Croquet Players*) accentuates their isolation. Homer's more literal engraving of a similar subject, *New England Factory Life*—*«Bell Time,»* was published in «Harper's» on July 25, 1868, accompanying an article discussing Charles Dickens's views on the New England factory system and his favorable reactions to the workers' conditions in the mills of Lowell, Massachusetts.[1] It would seem that Homer did not agree with Dickens.

Judging from his own record, Homer did not think much of school, either. In *The Country School*, one of Homer's few paintings of an interior, the emphasis is still on the outdoors: The viewer's eyes are drawn through the open room directly past the fluttering window shades to the inviting landscape

On Abaco Island
Wood engraving, 2½" × 1¾"
(6.4 × 4.5 cm)
The Century Magazine
February 1887, p. 501
The Library of Congress, Washington, D.C.

beyond (see page 23). The teacher is situated before the center blackboard like a third opaque window, occupying a zone apart from the children. Homer achieved this ironic commentary by creating an air of oppression rather than by focusing on particulars. In doing so, he avoided the sentimentality and predictability of many of the genre painters of his day. The following year, he completed a smaller version of this painting, *New England Country School* (Addison Gallery of American Art), and took up the subject again in the engraving *Noon Recess*[2] a recess clearly not enjoyed by the lone barefoot boy or the annoyed teacher looking out the window.

As in the case of the man in the top hat in *The Croquet Players*, the same teacher-model is used in various works. This teacher, however, may have been of special interest to Homer. According to Lloyd Goodrich, there was one painting that Homer always kept on an easel in his studio: that of a brown-haired young woman asking the question, «Shall I Tell Your Fortune?»[3] It is thought that this woman was a schoolteacher in the town of Hurley, New York, a woman with whom Homer had had a love affair that ended in disappointment.[4] The breakup might have been caused by Homer's unstable financial situation. At the same time this occurred, the young woman disappeared from his work.

That this affair deeply affected his attitude toward women and society, there can be no question. In his youth, though reserved, he had a

(1) See Marianne Doezema, *American Realism and the Industrial Age.* Cleveland, Ohio: Cleveland Museum of Art, 1980, p. 36.
(2) *Harper's Weekly*, June 28, 1873, p. 549.
(3) Lloyd Goodrich, *op. cit.*, pp. 56-57.
(4) See Jean Gould, « The Love Affair of Winslow Homer,» *New York Public Library Bulletin*, 66 (September 1962), pp. 447-448.

normal social life. From this time on he became more and more unsociable, and his taste for solitude grew. And after a few years women were to disappear from his art.[1]

Children, a less emotionally complicated subject, became a focal point for much of his work in the 1870s. In the postwar period of increasing materialism and industrialization, in which the social and economic fabric of society was changing—a period described by Mark Twain as the « Gilded Age »—children were a reminder of a less worldly, more natural state of man. And as popular genre subjects since the 1840s, they were vehicles for sentimental or humorous storytelling pictures. Eastman Johnson and Charles Caleb Ward depicted them on the farm, while Currier and Ives published numerous homespun prints of them. Homer portrayed his children with an affection and realism shared by Mark Twain's « Tom Sawyer. » But a boy's world could be occasionally worrisome. In *Snap-The-Whip*, the children have emptied out the country schoolhouse behind (see page 21). Left to their own devices, the boys release their pent-up energy (made apparent in *The Country School*), while the girls wait off in the wings. For all their exuberance, their activity is restricted and strained; some are forced out, left groping toward the space beyond. Homer reworked this subject in various media—in a preliminary chalk drawing and two paintings done in 1872 (one in the Metropolitan Museum without the mountainous background and the falling figure; the other at the Butler Institute of American Art, which resembles the engraving). The friezelike arrangement of figures, used previously in *Prisoners from the Front*, reappears in the later work *The Carnival* (see page 31), and the detailed foreground is similar to that in *The Two Guides* of 1875 (see page 27).

Despite his paintings' popularity with the public, they were less enthusiastically received by critics, who found Homer's native American subject matter and his unusual palette, coarse textures, and lack of «finish» wanting. Henry James expressed this point of view in his review of 1875, while also aptly describing Homer's work:

> Before Mr. Homer's little barefoot urchins and little girls in calico sun-bonnets, straddling beneath a cloudless sky upon the national rail fence, the whole effort of the critic is instinctively to contract himself, to double himself up, as it were. . . . Mr. Homer goes in, as the phrase is, for perfect realism, and cares not a jot for such fantastic hairsplitting as the distinction between beauty and ugliness. . . . He is almost barbarously simple, and, to our eye, he is horribly ugly; but there is nevertheless something one likes about him. What is it? For ourselves, it is not his subjects. We frankly confess that we detest his subjects—his barren plank fences, his glaring, bald, blue skies, his big, dreary, vacant lots of meadows, his freckled, straight-

(1) Lloyd Goodrich, *op. cit.*, p. 57.

High Tide. Wood engraving, 9¼" × 12" (23.5 × 30.5 cm)
Every Saturday, August 6, 1870, p. 504
The Library of Congress, Washington, D.C.

haired Yankee urchins, his flat-breasted maidens, suggestive of a dish of rural doughnuts and pie. . . . He has chosen the least pictorial features of the least pictorial range of scenery and civilization; he has resolutely treated them as if they were pictorial. . . . Mr. Homer, has the great merit, moreover, that he naturally sees everything at one with its envelope of light and air. He sees not in lines, but in masses, in gross broad masses. . . .[1]

James was not alone in rejecting American culture. The American painter James Abbott McNeill Whistler (born two years before Homer) went so far as to deny his Lowell,

(1) Henry James, Jr., « On Some Pictures Lately Exhibited, » *Galaxy* (July 1875), pp. 90, 93-94.

The Life-Line, 1882-1883
Black and white chalk on paper
17½" × 11" (44.5 × 28 cm)
Cooper-Hewitt Museum
The Smithsonian Institution's National
Museum of Design, New York

Massachusetts, birthplace after he settled in Europe at the age of twenty-one. He was followed by numerous young artists who fled America in search of «real» culture and professional instruction.

Children were also the subject of many of Homer's earliest watercolors, a medium he took up seriously at the age of thirty-seven during the summer of 1873 in Gloucester. Of course, he had been exposed to watercolor painting at a young age, but his mother painted still lifes of flowers and birds. He became intrigued, however, with the possibilities of capturing the rapidly changing effects of light out of doors. For the better part of the century thus far, watercolor painting had been regarded as a female and amateurish pastime, suitable for young girls to learn at school and put aside when they married. Although John James Audubon's watercolors, *The Birds of America*, were a major contribution to art, these works were associated with a reproduction process in which they were first printed and then hand-colored. It was not until 1866, with the establishment of the American Society of Painters in Water Colors (later called the American Water Color Society) that the medium was recognized as an independent art form.

By the time Homer began working in watercolors, his interest in graphic illustration had waned considerably (probably due to its comparative restrictiveness and his own financial health), and it had all but ended by 1874. Even so, his approach to watercolors was graphic at first: The drawing was worked out in pencil, then finished in watercolor and gouache. But watercolors allowed for freer explorations in color and light with an intimacy and immediacy less attainable in oils. Using washes in crisp colors and allowing the white of the paper to come through, he achieved a bright and airy atmosphere in which the figures moved with greater ease. If these children did not necessarily relate to one another, at least they were not alienated by gaps in space, as in his oils. *The Berry Pickers* (see page 20),

UNDERTOW, 1886
Oil on canvas
$29\,^{13}/_{16}''\times47\,^{5}/_{8}''$
(75.8 × 121.7 cm)
The Sterling and
Francine Clark
Institute
Williamstown
Massachusetts

43

Fog Warning, 1885
Oil on canvas, 30″ × 48″ (76.2 × 121.9 cm)
Museum of Fine Arts, Boston. Otis Norcross Fund

Boys Wading (1873, Colby College Museum of Art), *Girls with Lobster* (1873, Cleveland Museum), and *The Green Dory* (1880, Boston Museum of Fine Arts) best express the fresh qualities of his early efforts. Also in the 1870s, he painted a rather odd series of shepherdesses dressed in costume and numerous works of farm life. As was customary, these subjects were reworked in other media: *The Berry Pickers* suffers slightly as an engraving, printed in «Harper's, » July 11, 1874, while *Sailing the Catboat* (1873, private collection) becomes more monumental in its oil version, *Breezing Up* (see page 33).

With *Breezing Up*, Homer turns his attention from the shore to the sea, a theme that increasingly predominated in his work. Here the environment continues to serve as a milieu for the activities of the figures, and, as in the earlier paintings, the sea itself remains associated with recreation. Yet in the darkening skies, the introduction of the adult casts a sobering tone that prefigures a shift in focus in the 1880s from children at play to men at work, from nature as a backdrop to nature as an active force—and finally as a subject itself. Through a system of counterbalances Homer created structural tension, reflected in the line of the limp sliding boy angled against the taut horizontal rope pulled by the determined adult. The listing sailboat is diagonally juxtaposed to the steadying straight horizon, while the far-off boat to the right expands the distance. This format is frequently used in later works.

Homer made the first of many trips to the Adirondacks in the fall of 1870, in the company of painters Eliphalet Terry and John Fitch. Most of these early stays were in the Keene Valley and Minerva, New York; late in the 1880s, he would go camping, hunting, and fishing with his brother Charles as charter members of the North Woods Club. Hunting was a popular sport and as a popular subject for paintings that reached a wide audience through distribution as lithographs and engravings. William Tylee Ranney painted backwoodsmen in the 1850s while Arthur Fitzwilliam Tait, a prominent Currier and Ives artist, published a series of hunting scenes in 1863. American artists, unlike their British counterparts, showed hunting as a wilderness activity of the common man—the work of frontiersmen, not the self-conscious pastime of aristocrats. For Homer, these Adirondack trips germinated thematic material for some of his greatest works, as he turned to the portrayal of ordinary working people and to the fragile mortality of wildlife subject to the forces of man and of nature. These works reached their peak in the 1890s.

In *The Two Guides*, Homer placed Adirondack locals «Old Mountain» Phelps and the younger Monroe Holt in the foreground center of what would otherwise have been a landscape portrait of autumnal light (see page 27). With the larger areas blocked out and the foreground flowers detailed in thick dabs of paint, he patterned the painting with natural decorative touches such as mist clouds that rise like women's veils, anticipating the sea spray in the paintings of the 1890s. This composition, in which two figures gaze beyond a meadow, takes on more mysterious implications when the subjects are American blacks in a cotton field, as in *The Cotton Pickers*.

In 1875, Homer returned to Virginia to paint a series of portraits of black life. American blacks in early-nineteenth-century genre paintings were stereotyped in a variety of ways: as passive objects of ridicule, asleep and taunted by children (as in works by William Sidney Mount and James Goodwyn Clonney); as signposts to indicate locale; or as strumming banjo players (in Eastman Johnson's famous *Old Kentucky Home*, 1859).[1] Probably influenced by the publication of Harriet Beecher Stowe's «Uncle Tom's Cabin» (1852), the mid-century slave began appearing as the persecuted victim of slave markets. Homer's Civil War illustrations of blacks tended to show stereotypes as well (the merry dancer in *Bivouac Fire* [see page 30] or the happy-go-lucky *Our Jolly Cook* [National Gallery]). But during Reconstruction, this changed; the work became sympathetic. In part this series was a continuation of his farm scenes. As in his *Song of the Lark* (1876, Chrysler Museum), in which a farmer, scythe in hand, stands enraptured in a field, he made laboring black women heroic (*The Cotton Pickers*, see page 28), much as Miller made the French peasant heroic.[2] No longer decorative, as in *Sunlight and Shadow* (see page 25) and *The Butterfly* (Cooper-Hewitt Museum), these women dominate the composition; the wistful gaze of *The Croquet Match* here turns defiant. These women are massive and sculptural, silhouetted against the horizon yet close to the picture surface, in isolation from one another yet demanding serious consideration. *Upland Cotton* (1887-1895, Munson-Williams-Proctor Institute) is a more delicate, Oriental version of this subject.

In the brilliantly colored *The Carnival*, two women sew the final touches on the central male's harlequin costume, observed by fascinated children (see page 31). Arranged in another friezelike formation (as in *Prisoners from the Front* and *Snap the Whip*), the exotic characters seem to play out a mysterious pantomime. No longer comic minstrels, these blacks are portrayed with arresting stature and dignity. A lone child, her head draped in white, stares in wonder at the central trio, who are cast in ritualistic poses, their faces darkened in shadow. They are separated by a characteristic spatial gap—here before a gate—that, instead of alienating them, creates a magnetic tension between them. The fence (a frequent structural device in Homer's farm pictures) and the darkened foliage and sky combine to press the figures to the foreground, heightening the bright colors of their attire. The still, shady atmosphere accentuates the perplexing character of this painting.

It may be that Homer as a proper New Englander found blacks exotically attractive—primal, earthy, and mysterious. In the late 1880s and the '90s his interest in them was transferred to tropical locales. During his Virginia trips, he was criticized by local Southerners for choosing blacks as subjects worthy of painting; nevertheless, these works were well received by contemporary critics. George W. Sheldon wrote:

(1) See Patricia Hills, *The Painter's America: Rural and Urban Life, 1810-1910.* New York: Praeger, 1974, pp. 19-23, 58-73.
(2) See Michael Quick, «Homer in Virginia,» *Los Angeles County Museum of Art Bulletin,* 24 (1978), p. 76.

Perils of the Sea, 1888
Etching on paper, 16⅜" × 21¾" (41.6 × 55.3 cm)
National Museum of American Art, Smithsonian Institution, Washington, D.C.

His negro studies, recently brought from Virginia, are in several respects — in their total freedom from conventionalism and mannerism; in their strong look of life, and in their sensitive feeling character — the most successful things that this country has yet produced. [1]

TRANSITIONAL WORKS

In the spring of 1881, at the age of forty-five, Homer set sail for England and settled in the little fishing village of Cullercoats, near Tynemouth and Newcastle, on the North Sea. Why he chose Cullercoats is not really known — little written record exists of this period of his

(1) George W. Sheldon, *American Painters*. New York: D. Appleton and Company, 1879, p. 29.

life—yet it proved to be a major turning point in his career. He had devoted the previous summer entirely to watercolors, observing the finer subtleties of changing light and weather on Gloucester harbor while he stayed offshore on Ten Pound Island, Massachusetts, with the lighthouse keeper. Perhaps this physical isolation combined with a deepening interest in seaside atmospheric conditions stimulated him to make a more drastic move. Cullercoats had a marine painting tradition and, despite its remote location, was known to American artists.[1] The dramatic lives of its hardy fisherfolk inspired some of contemporary England's foremost painters, among them Frank Holl, William Quiller Richardson, Thomas Hook, and Charles Henry. Homer might also have been attracted to these heroic working people and to the other artists working there.

Although he lived alone in Cullercoats in a secluded cottage, his studio was pivotally located near the Brigade Watch House, featured prominently in *Perils of the Sea* (see page 47), and numerous other works. He worked mostly in watercolors, developing a change in style: Bright colors became more muted, hard lines softened, and figures became fuller. This partly had to do with the diffused English light, and with a shift in subject matter. He focused mainly on the Cullercoats women, their men anonymously relegated to the background or set offstage, unseen but anticipated. Homer ignored the fashionable women of the summer resorts nearby, and chose this hardworking, sturdy lot: women who took over the necessary chores when their husbands landed with the day's catch. Their weightier lives seem manifested in their forms. Such a change was already intimated in *The Cotton Pickers*, but now Homer has eliminated delicate detailing in the landscape. Grouped in twos and threes, they wait at the edge looking out to sea, not wistful (*The Croquet Match*) or self-possessed (*Long Branch, New Jersey*), but anxious and fearful (*Perils of the Sea*). This sense of anxiety in the latter work is revealed through unusually expressionistic handling: in the body language of the two women steeled against the elements (one's apron blows in the storm unornamentally, like a solid thing); in the cluster of readied men; and in the horizontal banding of the walkway, sea, and turbulent sky. In the original watercolor version of 1881 (Sterling and Francine Clark Institute), Homer included a railing along the walkway; its absence in the etching accentuates the women's vulnerability. *A Voice from the Cliffs* of 1883 (private collection) depicts a trio of women in a more conventionally romantic, pre-Raphaelite pose. *Inside the Bar, Tynemouth* (see page 34) portrays a stoic fisherwoman silhouetted against the horizon at the apex of a triangle, an anchor that unites the boats on either side, reinforced stylistically by the obvious repetition of curves. *The Life Boat* (see page 73), the drawing from *The Wreck of the «Iron Crown»* of 1881, was taken from an actual incident that occurred in the fall of that year, and is one of Homer's earliest examples of rescue work, a theme that preoccupied him later in the decade.

---

(1) For a discussion of Cullercoats and its artistic heritage see William H. Gerdts, « Winslow Homer at Cullercoats, » *Yale University Art Gallery Bulletin*, (Spring 1977), pp. 21-23.

EIGHT BELLS, 1886
Oil on canvas, 25 3/16" × 30 1/8" (64 × 76.5 cm)
Addison Gallery of American Art
Phillips Academy, Andover, Massachusetts

At Sea—Signalling a Passing Steamer
Wood engraving, 11⅝″ × 8¾″ (29.6 × 22.3 cm)
Every Saturday, August 8, 1871, p. 321
The Library of Congress, Washington, D.C.

SUNLIGHT ON THE COAST, 1890
Oil on canvas, 30¼″ × 48½″ (76.9 × 123.3 cm)
The Toledo Museum of Art, Ohio. Gift of Edward Drummond Libbey

At Cullercoats, Homer became aware of the power of the sea as a force itself and as it affected the lives of the men and women whose survival (and mortality) was inextricably bound to it. Their valiant struggles amidst the drama of nature's turbulence thematically inspired the course of his work. It is generally thought that Homer visited Cullercoats in 1881 and 1882. (Sometime in 1881 he visited London, where he completed an impressionistic watercolor of the *Houses of Parliament*, now at the Hirschhorn Museum) However, one Cullercoats resident had a differing recollection, indicating that he «had intended to stay only three months but loved the village and fisherfolk so much he remained for three years.»[1]

MATURE WORKS

Following his return to New York, Homer decided to move away for good to Prout's Neck, an isolated point on the Maine coast not far from Portland, where he settled for the rest of his life. He had first seen Prout's Neck in 1875, when he visited his younger brother, Arthur, who was honeymooning there with his bride. Now, eight years later, it must have seemed on ideal place to transplant his Cullercoats work to a Yankee location, free from distraction. His older brother, Charles, instigated the purchase of the property where he, Winslow, and their parents would relocate, hoping to develop the area into a summer resort. While the rest of the family settled into the main house, called the Ark, Homer claimed what formely had been a stable and redesigned it into a studio. Its second-floor balcony overlooked the rocky cliffs to the sea; along the cliffs was a public pathway he could travel to study the sea from various vantage points.

While still at Cullercoats, Homer had become interested in rescue operations, evident in *The Life Boat* and in *Watching the Tempest* (1881, Fogg Art Museum, Cambridge University). During the summer of 1883, he traveled to Atlantic City, New Jersey, to observe a demonstration of the breeches buoy. In *The Life-Line* (see page 41), this apparatus is used to rescue a woman passenger from a foundering boat, visible only by its torn sail and snapped line (on the left). The guardsman in the study for this work is looking away (see page 40). For the painting, Homer added further emphasis by completely obscuring his face with the hapless woman's tattered shawl. An inner tension results from the extremely physical but nonvisual interaction between the figures, shown from the male point of view—from looking but not touching (*The Croquet Players*), to touching but not looking. This is further dramatized by the (characteristic) introduction of red and by the highly activated brushstroke. According to Philip Beam, Homer could not get any of the local Maine girls to model in this seductive pose, so he resorted to fastening a small manikin on a bird perch that functioned as the buoy.[2]

(1) Quoted in William H. Gerdts, *op. cit.*, p. 26.
(2) See Philip C. Beam, *Winslow Homer at Prout's Neck*. Boston: Little, Brown, 1966, p. 64.

Study for Undertow, No. 2
1886
Pencil on paper
5" × 7³/₁₆" (12.7 × 19.5 cm)
The Sterling and
Francine Clark Institute
Williamstown, Massachusetts

Homer sent this work to the National Academy of Art exhibition in 1884, where on opening day a prominent collector bought it for twenty-five hundred dollars.[1] The image was so popular that Homer decided to reproduce it in an etching. The 1884 version closely follows the painting except that the elements on either side have been compressed, eliminating the ship's sail and the shoreline. In the 1889 version, the figure is reversed and the overall design is so much more decorative that Homer changed the title to *Saved* (see page 41).

Undertow (see pages 42-43), Homer's other female-rescue painting, was based on an incident that occurred during the same visit to Atlantic City in 1883. To achieve a realistic effect, he had a seventeen-year-old Maine girl pose for the preliminary sketches while her brother splashed buckets of water on her.[2] Homer tried a number of arrangements for the figures (see the drawings on pages 54 and 55), finally settling on a particularly classical friezelike formation, reminiscent of the Parthenon's East Pediment, in which their heads are again turned away from each other. The result is a bold and dramatic statement where the men seem denied what the women are allowed: As in *The Life-Line*, their eyes are hidden from the sensual poses of the women. The women, although clothed, seem as naked as the men; their wet garments cling to emphasize their voluptuous forms. And the force of the sea is shown as the deep well of a wave behind, drawing them back into danger, while

(1) See Lloyd Goodrich, *The Graphic Art of Winslow Homer*. New York: Museum of Graphic Art, 1968, p. 13.
(2) Philip C. Beam, *op. cit.*, p. 80.

breaking foam smooths around them.   Homer introduced a fuller palette here than in his oil paintings of the last few years, one that does not appear again for a while.   Shown at the National Academy in 1887, the painting received mixed reviews.

If women are relegated to the shoreline—defenseless when out at sea—men are cast adrift in boats—alone, with no landmarks in sight, struggling heroically against the treacheries of the elements. *Fog Warning* (see page 44) shows the plight of the lone fisherman who has drifted off course in an impending storm.   He is captured in stillness, in between motions, at the moment he assesses his fate—the critical distance between his dory and the safety of the schooner in the distance.   He is made universal by his anonymity, cast in an ominously glowing light that silhouettes forms, reducing all extraneous detail in modulated, unifying tones.   Man is integrated with his environment, yet isolated and subject to its indifference. The painting is a mature *Breezing Up*, a composite of countertensions and rising light and dark patterned forms, capsuled in the threatening fog overhead that connotes danger like the ragged shawl of *The Life-Line*.   In order to sketch this composition, Homer had a fisherman

Study for Undertow
No. 3, April 1886
Pencil on paper
5³⁄₄″ × 7¹⁄₄″
(14.6 × 18.5 cm)
The Sterling and
Francine Clark Institute
Williamstown
Massachusetts

model in a dory beached up on the sand. The original title, *Halibut Fishing*, was changed several years later.

In *Lost on the Grand Banks* (1886, Los Angeles County Museum), two fishermen rock helplessly in a swelling, vast sea, with no trace of land or assistance in sight. *The Herring Net* (Art Institute of Chicago) is based on a series of sketches made in 1884, when an unexpected school of herring swam into the area near Prout's Neck, attracting a fishing fleet.[1] Homer had a local boy row him right out to the sight so he could observe the incident close up. The men, whose faces are obscured by hats (a device used in *Undertow*), wrest the fish from the sea in a swell of heroic movement. *Eight Bells* is a variation in this series of paintings showing men at work (see page 49). Dressed in oilskins, the sailors have emerged on to the ship's deck to sight their course following a storm. The figure to the left holds a sextant to the barely visible sun, which breaks through a thick chiaroscuro of clouds. Through this dramatic atmosphere, touches of light reflect off their foul-weather gear. These archetypal men, faces obscured, are mere actors in the unfolding drama of nature—the sea and the changing effects of light.

To avoid jury duty, Homer left Prout's Neck in the fall of 1884 and made his first trip to the tropics that winter, spending his time in Florida, Nassau, and Santiago, Cuba. His work from these locales shows his fascination with the local flora (particularly evident in his palm tree studies of the 1890s), in the daily life of the native blacks, and in the architecture of various towns. Above all, he studied the play of the brilliant and bleached light as it reflected off water and walls, and the movement of clouds over the water. Using purer, brighter colors than in his oil paintings, he allowed the white paper to show through the pigment. Although seemingly spontaneous, pencil sketches are evident on the surface; there is a distinct sense of underlying structure in these works, in which the horizontal line often predominates.

Glass Windows, Bahamas (see page 36) brings to mind the studies of rock formations at Etretat on the Normandy coast done by French painters in the 1870s and '80s. In Courbet's oils of Etretat (1869-1870), a palpable landscape view is built with feathery strokes as a declaration of the form and mass of the rock; in Monet's views (1883-1886), the rock formation is an integral part of the surrounding atmosphere. Homer explored the structure itself, how it seemed at once material and immaterial set against variegated clouds in radiant tropical light. He conceptually played with the «window» by imposing scaled cliffs in a foreground wedge so that the band of sea must be viewed at an angle and the eye is continually brought forward to the jutting rocks and the pentimento figure at their edge. Everything around the structure seems incidental to it. This rock formation also compares to *Arched Rock, Capri* (1848), a more fanciful work by Jasper J. Cropsey, who was a member of the watercolor society to which Homer belonged.

(1) Philip C. Beam, *ibid.*, pp. 66-68.

A Summer Night, 1890
Oil on canvas, 29⅞″ × 39¾″ (76 × 101 cm)
Palais de Tokyo, Paris

Paddling at Dusk, 1892
Watercolor on paper, 15⅛″ × 21⅜″ (38.4 × 54.3 cm)
Memorial Art Gallery, University of Rochester, New York
Anonymous gift

58

ROWING HOME, 1890
Watercolor on paper, 13¾″ × 19⅞″ (35 × 50.5 cm)
The Phillips Collection, Washington, D.C.

DEER DRINKING, 1892
Watercolor on paper, $14\frac{1}{16}'' \times 20\frac{1}{16}''$ (36.7 × 51 cm)
Yale University Art Gallery, New Haven, Connecticut
The Robert W. Carle Fund

THE FALLEN DEER, 1892
Watercolor on paper, $13\frac{3}{4}'' \times 19\frac{3}{4}''$ (34 × 50.2 cm)
Museum of Fine Arts, Boston. Charles Henry Hayden Fund

THE END OF THE HUNT, 1892
Watercolor on paper, 15¼″ × 21½″ (36.7 × 54.6 cm)
Bowdoin College Museum of Art, Brunswick, Maine

61

TROUT FISHING, LAKE ST. JOHN, QUEBEC, 1895
Watercolor on paper, 11″ × 19¾″ (28 × 50.2 cm)
Museum of Fine Arts, Boston. William Wilkins Warren Fund

A Good Pool, Saguenay River, 1895
Watercolor over pencil sketch, 9¾″ × 18⅞″ (24.7 × 48 cm)
The Sterling and Francine Clark Institute
Williamstown, Massachusetts

Fox Hunt, 1893
Oil on canvas, 38″ × 68½″ (96.5 × 174 cm)
The Pennsylvania Academy of the Fine Arts, Philadelphia
Temple Fund Purchase

In Santiago, Cuba, Homer became fascinated with the play of light on architecture and produced a series of street scenes in which surface, pattern, and structural interplay of the buildings take precedence over the activities of the people. *Spanish Flag, Santiago de Cuba* (1885, Philadelphia Museum of Art) is a particularly abstract geometric composition painted with a broad swatch of vibrant color.

Between 1889 and 1894, Homer visited the Adirondacks almost every summer, often in the company of his brother Charles. Here he painted in watercolor what he saw and knew: hunters and their quarry, fishermen and their catch, in forests and on mountain lakes. There is a special attention to the singularity of forms always present in Homer's work and in these Adirondack pictures there is a particular feeling for isolated figures in this pristine setting. Animals are endowed with an ineffable sense of privacy, an alertness, and a dignity often not afforded people. In these hunting watercolors he explores by detached observation the implicit issue of mortality—how fate is played out in the hands of nature and in the hands of man. As has previously been discussed, hunting paintings enjoyed a certain popularity in nineteenth-century America. These were primarily genre paintings, in which the focus was on the act of the hunt or its aftermath, shown from the point of view of the huntsman either aiming at or displaying his quarry. Homer had composed a variation of this in his Civil War *Sharpshooter.* In the 1890s, he painted a series of watercolors that focused on the hunted, shown at the edge of fate, at the telling moment between life and death. In some works he showed the sequence of the kill as elements of a series of events; in others, its singular instantaneity.

An October Day (1889, Sterling and Francine Clark Institute) appears as an autumnal mountain landscape in splattered cadmium reds, mustards, washed gray-blues and greens reflected in crystalline blue water. But centered in the foreground is a swimming deer, the focus of a grim drama unfolding. One senses the quiver of its nose pressed against the picture plane, its animal awareness as it flees. It forms the apex of a triangle with its barely visible mortal enemies, a boy in a boat to the left and his hunting dog entering the water on the right. *Hound and Hunter* (1892, National Gallery) brings the elements closer; *After the Hunt* (1892, Los Angeles County Museum of Art) and the longer-viewed *End of the Hunt* (see page 61) show the conclusion.[1] What is described in these works is a customary method of hunting at that time. Hunters used dogs to chase the deer into the water close enough to their boats so they could kill the animals by drowning them. Alternatively, *A Good Shot* (1892, private collection) shows the deer at the moment of impact; *Deer Drinking* (see page 60) and *The Fallen Deer* (see page 60), before and after.[2] *Deer Drinking* is painted in unified, watery tones, with an intimacy that discourages human

(1) Henry Adams pointed to the connection between *An October Day* and *Hound and Hunter* in an article, « Mortal Themes: Winslow Homer, » *Art in America*, 71 (February 1983), p. 113.
(2) Theodore E. Stebbins, Jr., is credited for first pointing to the connection between *Deer Drinking* and *The Fallen Deer* in Henry Adams, *ibid.*, p. 122, note 2.

High Cliff, Coast of Maine, 1894
Oil on canvas, 30⅛″ × 38¼″ (76.5 × 97 cm)
National Museum of American Art, Smithsonian Institution
Washington, D.C. Gift of William T. Evans

THE ARTIST'S STUDIO IN AN AFTERNOON FOG, 1894
Oil on canvas, 24″ × 30″ (61 × 76.2 cm)
Memorial Art Gallery, University of Rochester, New York
R. T. Miller Fund

intrusion. Yet the viewer is allowed close enough to sense the softness and warmth of the animal's rounded belly against the fallen tree. The deer's alertness suggests a certain awareness of the unseen. In *The Fallen Deer*, the full weight of the body is nose-dived into the stream — its beady eye now lifeless. Its fragile foreleg juts up awkwardly while the head and tail fall in opposition; throughout there is an interplay between softness and brittleness, the belly, the tail, and the bones. In the clearing, bright color is introduced, suggesting the gunshot and blood, reflected in the pool of water by the animal's head. Remarkably, Homer is able to capture these moments subtly with an absence of sentimentality, with the eye of a naturalist. For his series of watercolors involving Adirondack guides, *Adirondack Guide* (1894, Boston Museum of Fine Arts), *The End of the Hunt*, and *Guide Carrying Deer* (1891, Portland Museum of Art, Maine), Homer would often sketch his subject on the spot and complete the work back in Maine, using separate retinues of models as stand-ins for one another.[1] According to Homer's nephew Charles, the setting for many of the Adirondack studies was the Sanctuary and pond called Great Massacre Pond near Prout's Neck.[2]

A fishing enthusiast all his life, he naturally chose various aspects of the sport as subjects for innumerable watercolors in Florida and Canada. Some of the most compelling are those in which the singular beauty of the fish is celebrated in paintings where action contradictorily borders on still life. *Jumping Trout* (1889, Portland Museum of Art, Maine) isolates the fish in flight, tracing its projectile downward over a delicate, crimson fly, showing it majestic even as it is victimized. *Fish and Butterflies* is an even more decorative work of Oriental sensibility (see page 77). It displays a yellow perch and two monarch butterflies painted in crisp, vibrant colors in nonreferential space. In *A Good Pool, Saguenay River*, Homer played with scale, compressed space, and abandoned logic altogether to show the experience of the fish (see page 63). Dumb, yet triumphant, it glides over the water while the small men below work feverishly to lure it in.

While in Quebec, Homer fished the Saguenay River (*A Good Pool*) and Lake St. John, other favorite remote woodland areas. His series of monochrome watercolors done in 1895, *Trout Fishing, Lake St. John, Province of Quebec* (see page 62), *Two Men in a Canoe* (Portland Museum of Art, Maine), and *Three Men in a Canoe* (private collection), show a remarkable affinity to sepia photographs. With a fluid wash and touches of China white, he conveyed the placid quality of a mirror-surfaced wilderness lake. Homer began taking pictures on fishing trips in Florida with a small box camera his brother Charles gave him.[3] Even before owning it, he showed a photographic eye in his ability to capture a particular moment in a series of actions, as in *Fog Warning*, or to depict a sequence of unfolding actions, as in *The Conch Divers* (1885, Minneapolis Institute of Arts). It is interesting to

(1) See Philip C. Beam, *op. cit.*, p. 102.
(2) *Ibid.*, p. 101.
(3) *Ibid.*, p. 34.

THE GULF STREAM, 1899
Oil on canvas, 28⅛″ × 48⅛″ (71.4 × 124.8 cm)
The Metropolitan Museum of Art, New York
Catharine Lorillard Wolfe Collection

note that when he did take photographs, they were not to freeze action but to record a scene, to be used as a reference tool for completing work when he returned home.

Rowing Home (see page 59) is another unusual watercolor showing barely discernible men in the midst of beautiful natural surroundings—here, a lake in Florida at sunset. Painted in a fluid wash, the work appears impressionistic, comparable to Claude Monet's *Impression, Sunrise* (1873) and his later *Waterloo Bridge, Sun in the Fog* (1903). *Blown Away* (see page 35) shares a delicacy of handling and airiness with *Rowing Home* in a more haunting, orientalized composition. The curving pattern found in *Inside the Bar, Tynemouth* is here less contrived, indicating Homer's growing skill in expressing moods and atmosphere with fewer referential elements. This sailing dory reappears as a detail in Homer's oil painting *Summer Squall* (1904, Sterling and Francine Clark Institute).

Back at Prout's Neck in the summer of 1890, Homer completed watercolors of his palm tree series begun in Florida (see *St. John's River, Florida*, page 79) and made the preliminary charcoal sketch for his painting *A Summer Night* (see page 57). The painting was inspired by a moonlit night on which his family and some local residents gathered on the rocks to watch the play of light on the ocean.[1] The two dancing figures were added later. The juxtaposition of this «moondance,» cast in cool, vaporous light, to the defined, silhouetted figures who jut out from the rocks creates an eerie, irrational atmosphere. The tiny red light on the horizon from the lighthouse on Wood's Island appears in Homer's other moonlit seascape, *Moonlight, Wood's Island Light* (Metropolitan Museum) of 1894. *A Summer Night* was shown at the Paris Exposition of 1900, where it was awarded a gold medal and was purchased by the French government. Although he subsequently received other comparable awards, Homer took special pride in this medal and always carried it with him.[2]

It was in the decade of the 1890s that Homer began the great series of marine paintings for which he is well known. In these works he observed the sea itself as a powerful expression of nature, without, for the most part, the intrusion of man. These works are meticulously observed at differing times of day in differing weather conditions, with a scientist's demand for accuracy. Seascapes, of course, were painted throughout the nineteenth century, mostly as historical or romantic renderings of shipwrecks in which man was cast afloat in the whirlwind wrath of God, or, as in Luminist paintings, as vehicles for the contemplation of God's presence. In the latter part of the century, as science increasingly prevailed, the presence of God began to disappear from paintings. These works were usually based on direct observation rather than imagination, without the moralizing overtones. The painter himself could then step in as the intermediary between nature and the viewer, and this was often done through thick, vigorous brushwork as evidence of the painter's hand. In Homer's

(1) *Ibid.*, p. 89.
(2) See Lloyd Goodrich, *Winslow Homer.* New York: Whitney Museum of American Art and Macmillan, 1944, p. 167.

case, the direct observation of changing natural conditions, of painting what he actually saw, has its roots in the Barbizon plein air approach and in Courbet's realism that led to Impressionism. Homer's approach was too bound to material form to allow for the insubstantiality of the Impressionists' renderings. Beyond the individual flicks and patterns of light and color, he saw nature as a force and challenge.

In *Sunlight on the Coast* (see page 52), he captured the suction force of a wave as it funnels in on itself, spewing foam and bursting in a spray, not unlike the cloud formations and scarves of his earlier periods. Built in four diagonal stages, the composition emphasizes the vastness of the sea and its interplay with the seemingly insignificant shore. In *Northeaster* (see page 74), the experience is more immediate as the pounding surf culminates in a translucent spray of whites, grays, and greens. The foreground rock is described in a restricted palette of thickly applied patches of color, while the churning foam is a heavy white impasto. Here, the materiality of sea and earth is felt. *West Point, Prout's Neck* is painted in a broader, streaked brush and composed with weighty horizontal

Tree Roots on a Hillside, Prout's Neck, 1885
Charcoal, white gouache on gray paper, 11¾" × 23⅝" (29.8 × 59.2 cm)
Cooper-Hewitt Museum, The Smithsonian Institution's National
Museum of Design, New York. Gift of Charles Savage Homer

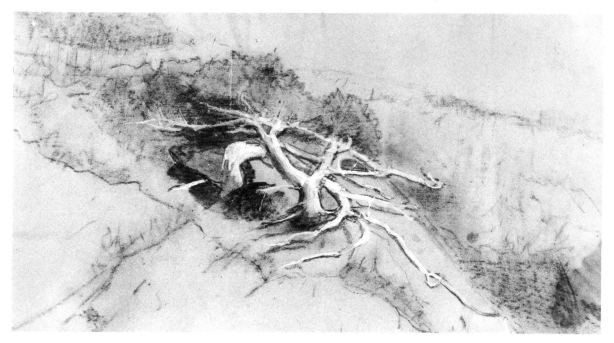

THE WRECK, 1896
Oil on canvas, 30″ × 48″ (76.2 × 122 cm)
Museum of Art, Carnegie Institute
Pittsburgh, Pennsylvania
Purchase from Winslow Homer

▷

*The Life Boat (The Wreck of the
« Iron Crown »), 1881
Black chalk, black wash
white gouache on paper
13¹⁵/₁₆″ × 19¹/₁₆″ (35.4 × 48.4 cm)
Cooper-Hewitt Museum
The Smithsonian Institution's National
Museum of Design, New York*

bands, suggesting fire and ice (see page 75). He described how the painting's light quality was achieved:

> The picture is painted *fifteen minutes* after sunset—not one minute before—as up to that minute the clouds over the sun would have their edges lighted with a brilliant glow of color—but now (in this picture) the sun has got behind their immediate range and *they are in shadow.* The light is from the sky in this picture. You can see that it took many days of careful observation to get this (with a high sea and tide just right).[1]

Despite these exacting observations, the painting is ornamentally decorated with a characteristic flourish of sea spray that has the flat, descriptive quality of a Japanese woodcut. By the same token, it took Homer a period of two years to find the right weather conditions to complete *Early Morning after the Storm at Sea* (1902, Cleveland Museum of

(1) *Ibid.,* p. 165.

NORTHEASTER, 1895
Oil on canvas, 34⅜″ × 50¼″ (87.3 × 127.5 cm)
The Metropolitan Museum of Art, New York·
Gift of George A. Hearn

WEST POINT, PROUT'S NECK, 1900
Oil on canvas, 30 1/16" × 48 1/8" (76.4 × 122.2 cm)
The Sterling and Francine Clark Institute
Williamstown, Massachusetts

Art), a luminous painting that also shows the sea in a calmer state. In *Winter Coast* (1890, Philadelphia Museum of Art) the battle of the elements shifts in focus to the rocky cliffs where man plays an insignificant role in the midst of a barren landscape pummeled by the sea. Homer spent many harsh New England winters alone in his studio painting; the desolation at this time of year is expressed in his paintings. In the more decorative and contemplative *Coast in Winter* (1892, Worcester Art Museum), the only trace of man is his footsteps in the snow.

The rigorous, rocky coast looms upwards in *High Cliff, Coast of Maine* (see page 66), where man is of little consequence in the interplay of unleashed natural forces. Compared with *Long Branch, New Jersey*, it is apparent how dramatically Homer's concerns have changed. The sea is no longer something to play in, or stroll by, but something to be mindful of, fear, and respect; no longer sun-drenched and bright, but moody and unpredictable. This work was painted from an actual point on Prout's Neck called High Cliff. In September of 1901 Homer wrote to the Knoedler Gallery in New York about this painting: «I have not painted anything this summer, but I have a picture that you have never seen in the shape that it is now in, and it is very beautiful in my opinion....»[1] The following year, annoyed that it had not sold, he wrote: «Why do you not sell that "High Cliff" picture? I cannot do better than that. Why should I paint?»[2]

In the winter of 1898, Homer made his second trip to Nassau. There he experimented with purer, more vibrant colors in a clearer light, building the picture through contrasting tonal values with a sensitivity to light and dark areas he had developed in his early printing days: «I have never tried to do anything but get the proper relationship of values; that is, the values of dark and light and the values of color. It is wonderful how much depends upon the relationship of black and white....» He continued studying tropical landscape, the hot sun reflected in the turquoise water, the balmy air, and with predominantly horizontal line reinforced the calmer surrounding atmosphere and the sense of open space. For example, *A Wall, Nassau* (see page 80) is a condensed *On the Way to Market* (1885, Brooklyn Museum) brought to life. In the latter, a figure is set before a stucco wall as a bland reference point, barely discernible in her surroundings. The wall is a familiar structural device replacing the picket fences that appeared behind figures in Homer's paintings of the 1870s. By the 1890s, Homer had managed to eliminate the figure altogether from almost all of his landscapes. In *A Wall, Nassau*, he portrayed the riotous poinsettia bursting above the ordinary stucco wall behind which more modulated foliage and the expansive sky and sea are found. The composition approaches abstraction and does not pretend to be about anything but tropical color and light in a spatial arrangement. *Hurricane, Bahamas* (1898, Metropolitan Museum) shows a different mood, a cloudy time before the onset of

(1) *Ibid.*, p. 172.
(2) *Ibid.*, p. 172.
(3) *Ibid.*, p. 159.

FISH AND BUTTERFLIES, 1900
Watercolor over pencil, 14$^1/_2$″ × 20$^{11}/_{16}$″ (36.8 × 52.2 cm)
The Sterling and Francine Clark Institute, Williamstown, Massachusetts

PALM TREES, FLORIDA, 1904
Watercolor on paper
19⅛″ × 13½″ (48.5 × 34.3 cm)
Museum of Fine Arts, Boston
Bequest of John T. Spaulding
◁

ST. JOHN'S RIVER, FLORIDA, 1890
Watercolor on paper
14″ × 20″ (35.6 × 51.8 cm)
Private collection
Courtesy Acquavella Galleries, New York

Cuban Hillside, 1885
Pencil, white chalk
white gouache on gray paper
10¹³/₁₆″ × 17⁷/₁₆″ (29.9 × 44.2 cm)
Cooper-Hewitt Museum
The Smithsonian Institution's National
Museum of Design, New York
Gift of Charles Savage Homer

◁

A Wall, Nassau, 1898
Watercolor and pencil on paper
14³/₄″ × 21¹/₂″ (37.5 × 55.5 cm)
The Metropolitan Museum of Art, New York
Amelia B. Lazarus Fund

◁

The Turtle Pound, 1898
Watercolor over pencil
14¹⁵/₁₆″ × 21³/₈″ (38 × 54.2 cm)
The Brooklyn Museum, New York
Sustaining Membership Fund
A. T. White Memorial Fund
A. Augustus Healy Fund

a tropical storm. The work is literally built architecturally with blocky houses, yet it is delicate in its sensitive rendering of palms.

The bleached wooden pen in the *Turtle Pound* (see page 80) becomes the organizing device for Homer's strangely iconic portrayal of black Bahamians in an ordinary yet seemingly ritualized activity. (Turtles were kept in these pens as food reserves.) Ironically, these men's forms are structurally more substantial than the wall built between them; their faces are particularly portraitlike and painterly, while their skin tones are differentiated. Nonetheless, the figures serve as center-pieces for a description of the play of light on water that is layered in greens, teal, and royal blue below clouds that seem pasted strips in gray-blue flourishes. Homer painted a number of portraits of blacks on this trip, including *Rum Cay* (1898-1899, Worcester Art Museum) and *Under the Coco Palm* (1898, Fogg Art Museum, Harvard University). In all of them the figures have an elusive quality, as if they exist on another level of awareness.

Girl on a Swing, 1879
Graphite on wove paper, $8^{5}/_{16}$" × $5^{1}/_{4}$"
(21.1 × 13.4 cm)
Cooper-Hewitt Museum
The Smithsonian Institution's National
Museum of Design, New York

Homer usually saved his most forceful statements for his oil paintings. In his enigmatic *The Gulf Stream* (see page 69) he combined two of his favorite themes by setting a stoic black man amid the treacherous elements. The idea for this work originated in his studies made during his previous trip to Nassau in 1885 and corresponds to previous marine-disaster paintings such as John Singleton Copley's *Brook Watson and the Shark* (1778) and J. M. William Turner's *The Slave Ship* (1840). The work is peculiarly romantic and illustrative for so late in Homer's career, but nonetheless has a psychological power achieved through the interplay of passive-aggressive elements. Nature appears in full force: Sharks with razor-sharp teeth churn in red-blotched water in the foreground; in the middle ground a wave breaks; and a waterspout looms on the distant horizon. This rampant activity is juxtaposed to the utter passivity of the prostrate man on the deck of his brokenmasted boat, cast to the fates, powerless and indifferent. Here man has given up the struggle.

At the request of the director of the Pennsylvania Academy of Fine Arts in Philadelphia («that the greatest American Art Exhibition can not open without an example from the greatest American artist»[1]), Homer sent *The Gulf Stream* for the exhibition of 1900 before it was finished. When completed, it went to Homer's New York gallery for his highest asking price of four thousand dollars.[2] It failed to sell. When asked for an explanation of the work, Homer replied:

> ...I regret very much that I have painted a picture that requires any description. The subject of this picture is comprised in *its title* and I will refer these inquisitive school ma'ms to Lieut. Maury. I have crossed the Gulf Stream *ten* times and I should know something about it. The boat and sharks are outside matters of very little consequence. *They have been blown out to sea by a hurricane!* You can tell these ladies that the unfortunate Negro who now is so dazed and parboiled will be rescued and returned to his friends and home, and ever after live happily.[3]

The painting was not sold until 1906.

Fox Hunt (see page 64), like *The Gulf Stream*, is a major oil painting based on themes previously explored in watercolor. Homer's numerous works on the hunt culminate in this stark exposition of

Two Girls on a Swing, 1879
Graphite on wove paper, 6¾" × 4⅛"
(17.1 × 10.4 cm)
Cooper-Hewitt Museum
The Smithsonian Institution's National
Museum of Design, New York

(1) Quoted in Natalie Spassky, *op. cit.*, p. 37.
(2) See Lloyd Goodrich, *op. cit.*, p. 162.
(3) *Ibid.*, p. 162.

the hunted as helpless victim at the cruel hands of nature: A fox floundering in the snow is about to be attacked by crows. Although similar in arrangement to Courbet's *Fox in the Snow* (1860), Homer's work is flattened and more direct. Simplified patterns form isolated silhouettes with all extraneous detail removed, as the focus placed asymmetrically creates a heightened graphic effect, reminiscent of Hiroshige's *Juman-tsubo Plain at Susaki, Fukagawa* (1858). The subtle tonal values are interrupted only by the sinister red dabs to the left, representing berries on delicate twigs. To compose *Fox Hunt*, Homer arranged dead crows as if in flight on a snowdrift outside his studio window and propped up a dead fox set in running position with sticks and strings.[1] Apparently, the bodies kept growing limp in the melting snow, and so Homer had one of the locals lure in real crows with corn so he could sketch them in flight.

Kissing the Moon (see page 85) is more enigmatic still, seemingly part real, part imagined. Painted in brighter colors than other men at sea oils, it depicts three apparently truncated men in a barely visible boat between two waves. The foreground wave slices their upper bodies on a diagonal so they appear like puppets bobbing behind a raked screen. The cresting wave that touches the moon in a «kiss» is parallel in design to Hokusai's *Great Wave off Kanawa*. It is unclear what these men are doing (Homer's nephew Charles was the model for the figure on the left), but they are characteristically obscured by hats, isolated from one another, and wrapped in their own thoughts. There is, moreover, an ominous sense of waiting as the sun sets in the cloud-streaked sky and the moon begins to rise.

The Wreck (see page 72) is a culminating work in the series of studies on rescue operations, harkening back to some of Homer's earliest Cullercoats works, such as *The Life Boat* (see page 73) and *The Wreck of the «Iron Crown»* (private collection). The painting is a concise statement of motion, struggle, and determination cast in monochromatic tones that subdue individual elements. The dynamic zigzag compositional lines force the eye through more pathways than the direct diagonal line of the earlier works. Part of the painting's power lies in the fact that Homer never showed the actual shipwreck itself, but built tension by revealing all the activity around it.

In 1898, when Homer was sixty-two, his father, whose care he had overseen all the years at Prout's Neck, died. Homer was invited the same year to join a group of artists, «Ten American Painters,» formed for exhibiting work. He replied, «You do not realize it, but I am too old for this work and I have already decided to retire from business at the end of the season.»[2] Always the tough practicalist, he chose to refer to his art as «business» and was in fact increasingly consumed in his later life by the details of selling his works. It may have been this kind of blackened mood, perhaps intimations of his own death, that influenced his darker, haunting late paintings.

(1) See Philip C. Beam, *op. cit.*, p. 109.
(2) Quoted in Lloyd Goodrich, *op. cit.*, p. 154.

KISSING THE MOON, 1904
Oil on canvas, 30″ × 40″ (76.2 × 101.7 cm)
Addison Gallery of American Art, Phillips Academy
Andover, Massachusetts

Searchlight on Harbor Entrance, Santiago de Cuba (1901, Metropolitan Museum of Art) is based on the event of the U. S. blockade of Santiago harbor during the Spanish-American War of 1898. Composed in a bare design, this painting exhibits deliberately depersonalized, unromantic subject matter chosen by Homer to portray a mood of solemnity, both eerie and melancholy. A meditative, eternal atmosphere pervades *Cape Trinity, Saguenay River* (see page 90), where the rounded, mountainous forms barely penetrate the velvety moonlit night.

In the early 1900s, Homer painted a series of watercolors on his Florida trips, concentrating on some of his favorite subjects, fishing and the lush vegetation of the Homosassa River region. Among the most beautiful studies is *Palm Trees, Florida*, a celebration of vibrant, even unlikely tropical colors in a concentrated still life format (see page 78). In the winter of 1905 Homer painted his last signed and dated watercolor, *Diamond Shoal* (IBM Collection). A comparison with *Breezing Up* can be made to see how Homer's handling of seafaring boats has evolved. All narrative elements have been eliminated, while the focus is directed to the interplay between the foreground schooner aggressively approaching the picture plane and the «Diamond Shoal» cuts across the horizon in the rear. His works have become finely honed.

Between the fall of 1905 and that of 1908, Homer produced no new work. When asked in July 1907 to grant an interview for an article about his painting, Homer replied, «Perhaps you think that I am still painting and interested in art. *That is a mistake.* I care nothing for art. I no longer paint. I do not wish to see my name in print again.»[1] Whether his attitude was due to ill health, disappointment at the reception of his latest work, or a failing in creativity is uncertain. In the spring of 1908, the Carnegie Institute featured twenty-two of his oils at its twelfth annual exhibition, the most complete survey of his work thus far held. That May, he suffered a cerebral hemorrhage, and in June he wrote to his brother Charles that he was now able to tie his necktie and hoped to be painting again soon.[2] By the beginning of the following month, he was well enough to return to the North Woods Club in the Adirondacks, surely a result of his Yankee iron will. In December of that year, he wrote his brother again that he was working on «a most surprising picture.»[3] That picture was *Right and Left* (see page 88). Remarkably reminiscent of Audubon's *American Golden-Eye* (1834) in form if not style or intent, it shows two ducks in midair at the brink of death. More than any of Homer's previous hunting pictures, this one jolts the viewer to the experiential level by showing the victims pressed flat against the picture plane at the moment of the blast's impact (a stray feather drifts to the right). The color tones are homogenized for concentrated effect, except for the connection drawn between

(1) Winslow Homer to Leila Mechlin, letter of July 1907. Quoted in Lloyd Goodrich, *op. cit.*, p. 188.
(2) Winslow Homer to Charles L. Homer, letter of June 4, 1908. Quoted in Philip C. Beam, *op. cit.*, p. 246.
(3) *Ibid.*, p. 246.

one duck's bright, still-open eye and the flash of the rifle. Despite the illusion of instantaneity, Homer has achieved more than a photographic record of an event to intimate an experience more metaphysical than real.

Insisting on accuracy to the very end, Homer had hired a man to row offshore and fire blank charges up a cliff where he watched so he could see what a shotgun blast looked like to someone under fire.[1]   The painting, originally untitled, was shown at the Knoedler

(1) For a discussion of how Homer created *Right and Left* and how it was subsequently titled, see Philip C. Beam, *op. cit.*, p. 249.

Fisherman in Quebec, 1895
Black and gray wash, white gouache, charcoal on gray paper
12" × 20 1/16" (30.6 × 50.9 cm)
Cooper-Hewitt Museum, The Smithsonian Institution's National
Museum of Design, New York

RIGHT AND LEFT, 1909
Oil on canvas, 28¼″ × 48¾″ (71.8 × 122.9 cm)
The National Gallery of Arts, Washington, D.C. Gift of the Avalon Foundation

Gallery in New York. A sportsman saw it and exclaimed, «Right and left,» a hunter's term for hitting two birds simultaneously, one with each barrel of a gun—and the painting was subsequently given its title. This painting is a more concise version of a theme hinted at but diffused in *Wild Geese* (1897, Portland Museum of Art, Maine). *Artist's Studio in an Afternoon Fog* (see page 67) is perhaps Homer's most personal work. And despite his protestations that he was not a hermit, it is a portrait of isolation, restraint, and detachment, elements common to the interaction between his figures as well as his manifestations of nature through landscape. He chose to present himself (at his home and workplace) through a thick, impenetrable fog, casting a barrier of diagonal rocks between the building and the viewer. In *Driftwood*, painted in 1909 (private collection), the figure seen from the back is in the viewer's position, barred from the open sea by an overturned log. Significantly, this is one of the few late paintings in which a figure is present. It could be that this figure, inexplicably appearing to have something still to do, is Homer himself. In his final statement on man's struggle with the elements, he allowed nature to speak calmly, leaving man stifled and mute. After he finished this painting, he deliberately smeared his palette and hung it up on his studio wall where it remained. On September 29, 1910, Homer died following a cerebral hemorrhage suffered earlier in the month.

Homer's life was devoted entirely to his art. His experiences and observations were recorded in his work, rearranged and interpreted to appear as truth and as discovered fact. His attitude toward working was, «I will paint only when I want to, and for my own pleasure.» [1] «Every condition must be favorable or I do not work and will not.» [2] His approach was that of a naturalist, studying the individual with an eye for the specific, transforming that essence into something unexplainable, even mythic. As his work matured, it lost all sense of date and time, assuming a quality of the present, ever-occurring in silence. His additional gift was his ability to distill forms almost to the point of abstraction while still retaining their factual appearance. His work verged on the subjective, touching twentieth-century themes of alienation and mortality with a probing depth counterbalanced by formal simplicity. Concerning his own legacy, he remarked, «You will see, in the future I will live by my watercolors.» [3]

His watercolors have a freshness and immediacy that know no time; although still representational, they celebrate color, light, and form in a truly modern sense. Ironically, it is his oil paintings that are most often seen. They express an elemental power and mystery that transcends the everyday realities of late twentieth-century to focus on pure experience.

(1) Winslow Homer to John W. Beatty. Quoted in Lloyd Goodrich, *op. cit.*, p. 170.
(2) Winslow Homer to Col. Briggs. *Ibid.*, p. 170.
(3) Quoted in Lloyd Goodrich, *ibid.*, p. 159.

Cape Trinity, Saguenay River, Moonlight, 1906-1907
Oil on canvas, 28½″ × 48″ (72.4 × 122 cm)
Private collection. Courtesy Museum of Fine Arts, Boston

BIOGRAPHY

1836   Winslow Homer was born in Boston on February 24, the son of Charles Savage Homer and Henrietta Maria Benson Homer.

1842   Homer's family moved to Cambridge, Massachusetts.

1854 or 1855   Apprenticed to John H. Bufford, lithographer, in Boston.

1857   Resigned from Bufford's and began his career as an independent illustrator. Worked from a rented studio in the « Ballou's Pictorial » building in Boston. First illustrations appeared in « Ballou's Pictorial » and « Harper's Weekly. »

1859   Moved to New York in the fall. Lived at 52 East Sixteenth Street and rented a studio on Nassau Street.

1860   Attended drawing class in Brooklyn and took night classes under Thomas Seir Cummings at the National Academy of Design.

1861   Moved to a studio in the New York University Building on Washington Square, where painter Eastman Johnson also worked. Studied oil painting with Frédéric Rondel. Spent the summer near Boston. In October, visited Civil War Army of the Potomac in Virginia as an artist-correspondent for « Harper's Weekly. »

1862   Returned to Virginia in the spring to cover the Peninsular Campaign. Completed his first adult oil painting, *The Sharpshooter.*

1863   Made occasional trips to the Virginia front and continued to produce war illustrations and paintings.

1864   Elected an Associate of the National Academy of Design.

1865   Elected a National Academician.

1866   Exhibited *Prisoners from the Front* at the National Academy of Design, the painting that firmly established his artistic reputation. Sailed for his first trip to Europe in the late fall.

1867   Lived in Paris, sharing a studio in Montmartre with artist Albert Warren Kelsey. Visited the Louvre and the Universital Exposition, where his paintings *Prisoners from the Front* and *The Bright Side* were on display. Returned to New York in the fall.

1868-1869   Summers in the White Mountains, New Hampshire.

1870   First known trip to the Adirondacks in the early fall. Stayed at a farm near Minerva, New York, with painters Eliphalet Terry and John Fitch.

1872   Moved to Tenth Street Studio Building in New York.

1873   Summer in Gloucester, Massachusetts, where he began painting watercolors.

1874   Summer in the Adirondacks.

1875   Last illustration published in « Harper's Weekly. » Spent the summer in York, Maine, and traveled to Petersburg, Virginia where he began his painting series of blacks, 1875-1879. First major watercolor exhibition at the American Water Color Society.

1877   Painted tiles and became a founding member of the Tile Club.

1878   Summer at Houghton Farm, Hurley, New York. May have had a love affair about this time.

1879   Summer in West Townsend, Massachusetts. Continued making watercolors and drawings of children.

1880   Summer on Ten Pound Island, Gloucester, Massachusetts.

1881   Second voyage to Europe in the spring. Settled in Cullercoats, England, near Tynemouth and Newcastle. Worked almost entirely in watercolors, painting the North Sea fishermen and their families. Visited London sometime during this period where he painted *Houses of Parliament.*

1882   Exhibited *Hark! The Lark* at the Royal Academy, London. Returned to New York in November.

1883   Visited Atlantic City, New Jersey, in early summer. Settled at Prout's Neck, Maine, that summer. Exhibited his English watercolors in Boston.

1884   Exhibited *The Life Line* at the National Academy of Design, New York. Sailed with fishing fleet to the Grand Banks. His mother died on April 27. Traveled to Nassau,

Bahamas, in December, his first trip to the tropics.

1885   First few months in Nassau and Cuba where he painted watercolors. Completed *Fog Warning* and *The Herring Net*.

1886   Spent January in Florida. Completed *Eight Bells, Lost on the Grand Banks,* and *Undertow* at Prout's Neck.

1887   Painted watercolors at Prout's Neck. Published Civil War sketches in the « Century » magazine. Exhibited *Undertow* at the National Academy of Design. No oil paintings dated 1887-1889.

1889   Summer and fall in the Adirondacks, painting watercolors.

1890   Winter in Florida painting watercolors. Exhibited Adirondack watercolors in Boston. Thomas B. Clark began collecting his work.

1891   Summer and fall in the Adirondacks.

1893   Exhibited fifteen paintings at the Columbian Exposition in Chicago and was awarded a gold medal for *The Gale. Fox Hunt* was shown at the Pennsylvania Academy of the Fine Arts in Philadelphia.

1896   Awarded $ 5,000 purchased prize for *The Wreck*, at the first International Exhibition at Carnegie Institute, Pittsburgh. Remained at Prout's Neck throughout the year.

1897   Second visit to Quebec in the summer.

1898   His father died on August 22. Spent the winter of 1898-1899 in Nassau, Bahamas.

1899   Returned to Prout's Neck and completed *The Gulf Stream*. The Clark collection was sold at auction in February. Sailed for Bermuda in December.

1900   Summer in the Adirondacks. Exhibited *Fox Hunt, High Cliff, Coast of Maine, The Lookout — « All's Well »,* and *A Summer Night* at Paris Exposition. Awarded a gold medal for *A Summer Night* which was purchased by the French Ministry of Fine Arts for the Luxembourg Palace Museum. Completed *On*

a Lee Shore, Eastern Point, Prout's Neck, and *West Point, Prout's Neck,* among his finest marine oils.

1901   Awarded gold medal for watercolors shown at Pan-American Exposition in Buffalo, New York. Spent the winter in Bermuda.

1902   Union League of New York exhibition of *Searchlight on Harbor Entrance, Santiago de Cuba,* his painting from the Spanish-American War of 1898. Last visit to Quebec. Awarded Temple gold medal for *Northeaster* and *High Cliff, Coast of Maine,* Pennsylvania Academy of the Fine Arts, and a gold medal for *Cannon Rock* at the Charleston Exposition, South Carolina.

1903   Winter of 1903-1904 in Florida, at Key West and the Homosassa River region, painting watercolors.

1904   Returned to Prout's Neck and completed *Kissing the Moon* and *Cape Trinity, Saguenay River.* Awarded gold medal for *Weather-Beaten* at the Louisiana Purchase Exposition in St. Louis.

1905   Spring in the Adirondacks and winter in Atlantic City. Completed *Diamond Shoal,* his last signed and dated watercolor. He produced no new works from the fall 1905 to the fall 1908.

1906   Suffered illness from the summer until almost year's end, and was unable to work. *The Gulf Stream* was purchased by the Metropolitan Museum of Art in New York for the highest purchase price he had ever received.

1908   Suffered paralytic stroke in May. Traveled to the Adirondacks in the summer for the last time. Began working on *Right and Left.*

1909   Completed *Right and Left* in January and *Driftwood,* his last painting, in November.

1910   Exhibited *The Gulf Stream* and *The Lookout — « All's Well »* at the American Art Exposition in Berlin and Munich. Died on September 29 at Prout's Neck, following a cerebral hemorrhage suffered earlier in the month.

SELECTED BIBLIOGRAPHY

ADAMS, Henry. « Mortal Themes: Winslow Homer, » *Art in America*, 71 (February 1983), pp. 112-126.

BEAM, Philip C. *Winslow Homer at Prout's Neck.* Boston: Little, Brown, 1966.

CIKOVSKY, Nicolai, Jr. « Winslow Homer's Prisoners from the Front, » *Metropolitan Museum Journal*, 12 (1977), pp. 155-172.

COX, Kenyon. *Winslow Homer.* New York, 1914.

CURRY, David Park. *Winslow Homer: The Croquet Game.* New Haven: Yale University Art Gallery, 1984.

DOEZEMA, Marianne. *American Realism and the Industrial Age.* Cleveland, Ohio: Cleveland Museum of Art, 1980.

DOWNES, William Howe. *The Life and Works of Winslow Homer.* Boston: Houghton, Mifflin, 1911.

FLEXNER, James Thomas. *The World of Winslow Homer, 1836-1910.* New York: Time Incorporated, 1966.

GARDNER, Albert Ten Eyck. Introduction, *Winslow Homer: A Retrospective Exhibition.* Washington, D.C. and New York: National Gallery of Art and Metropolitan Museum of Art, 1959.

—— *Winslow Homer, American Artist: His World and His Work.* New York: Clarkson Potter, 1961.

GELMAN, Barbara. Introduction, *The Wood Engravings of Winslow Homer.* New York: Crown, 1969.

GERDTS, William H. « Winslow Homer in Cullercoats, » *Yale University Art Gallery Bulletin*, 36 (Spring 1977), pp. 18-35.

GOODRICH, Lloyd. *American Watercolor and Winslow Homer.* Minneapolis: The Walker Art Center, 1945.

—— *The Graphic Art of Winslow Homer.* New York: Museum of Graphic Art, 1968.

—— *Winslow Homer.* New York: Whitney Museum of American Art and Macmillan, 1944.

—— *Winslow Homer.* New York: George Braziller, 1959.

—— *Winslow Homer.* New York: Whitney Museum of American Art, 1973.

GOULD, Jean. « The Love Affair of Winslow Homer, » New York: *Public Library Bulletin*, 66 (September 1962), pp. 444-448.

GROSSMAN, Julian. *Echo of a Distant Drum: Winslow Homer and the Civil War.* New York: Harry N. Abrams, 1974.

HANNAWAY, Patti. *Winslow Homer in the Tropics.* Richmond, Virginia: Westover, 1973.

HENDRICKS, Gordon. *The Life and Work of Winslow Homer.* New York: Harry N. Abrams, 1979.

HILLS, Patricia. *The Painter's America: Rural and Urban Life, 1810-1910.* New York: Praeger, 1974.

HOOPES, Donelson F. *Winslow Homer Watercolors.* New York: Watson-Guptill; Oxford: Phaidon, 1969.

JAMES, Henry, Jr. « On Some Pictures Lately Exhibited, » *Galaxy*, 20 (July 1875), pp. 90, 93-94.

KAPLAN, Sidney. « The Negro in the Art of Homer and Eakins, » *Massachusetts Review*, 7 (Winter 1966), p. 112.

KATZ, Leslie. « The Modernity of Winslow Homer, » *Arts*, 33 (February 1959), pp. 24-27.

NOVAK, Barbara. *American Painting of the Nineteenth Century: Realism, Idealism, and the American Experience.* Second edition. New York: Harper & Row, 1979.

QUICK, Michael. « Homer in Virginia, » *Los Angeles County Museum of Art Bulletin*, 24 (1978), pp. 61-81.

SHELDON, George W. *American Painters.* New York: D. Appleton and Company, 1879.

SPASSKY, Natalie. *Winslow Homer at the Metropolitan Museum of Art.* New York: Metropolitan Museum of Art, 1982.

STEIN, Roger B. *Seascape and the American Imagination.* New York: Clarkson N. Potter, 1975.

WILMERDING, John. *Winslow Homer.* New York: Praeger, 1972.

—— « Winslow Homer's English Period, » *American Art Journal*, 7 (November 1975), pp. 60-69.

Winslow Homer in the Adirondacks. Introduction by Lloyd Goodrich. Essay by James W. Fosburgh. Blue Mountain Lake, New York: Adirondack Museum, 1959.

RECENT EXHIBITIONS

1951 *Winslow Homer Illustrator.* Smith College Museum of Art, Northampton, Massachusetts; Williams College, Williamstown, Massachusetts. Catalogue by Mary Bartlett Cowdrey.

1959 *Winslow Homer: A Retrospective Exhibition.* Museum of Fine Arts, Boston; National Gallery, Washington, D. C.; Metropolitan Museum of Art, New York. Text by Albert Ten Eyck Gardner.

1963 *Yankee Painter. A Retrospective Exhibition of Oils, Watercolors and Graphics by Winslow Homer.* University of Arizona Art Gallery, Tucson. Text by William Steadman.

1964 *Homer and the Sea.* Mariners Museum, Newport, Virginia. Catalogue by William Francis.

1966 *Paintings of Winslow Homer at the Cooper Union Museum.* Ira Spanierman Gallery, New York. Introduction by Albert Ten Eyck Gardner.

1966 *Winslow Homer at Prout's Neck.* Bowdoin College Museum of Art, Brunswick, Maine. Introduction by Philip C. Beam.

1968 *Winslow Homer's Sub-Tropical America.* Jo and Emily Lowe Art Gallery, Miami University, Coral Gables, Florida.

1968 *The Graphic Art of Winslow Homer.* Museum of Graphic Art, New York. Foreword by Donald H. Karshan. Catalogue by Lloyd Goodrich.

1972 *Winslow Homer, 1836-1910. A Selection from the Cooper-Hewitt Collection.* Smithsonian Institution, Washington, D.C.

1972 *Winslow Homer, A Selection of Watercolors, Drawings and Prints.* Metropolitan Museum, New York; Albright-Knox Art Gallery, Buffalo, New York; Albany Institute of History and Art, New York. Catalogue by Natalie Spassky.

1973 *Winslow Homer.* Whitney Museum of American Art, New York. Catalogue by Lloyd Goodrich.

1977 *Winslow Homer's Florida. 1886-1909.* Cummer Gallery of Art. Jacksonville, Florida.

1977 *Winslow Homer.* Museum of Fine Arts, Boston.

1977 *Winslow Homer. Graphics from the Mavis P. and Mary Wilson Kelsey Collection.* Museum of Fine Arts, Houston, Texas. Catalogue by Mavis Parrott Kelsey.

1977-1978 *Winslow Homer in New England Collections.* Museum of Fine Arts, Boston.

1978 *Winslow Homer. Works on Paper.* Baltimore Museum of Art.

1979 *Winslow Homer. Drawings 1875-1885. Houghton Farm to Prout's Neck.* Jo and Emily Lowe Art Center, Syracuse University, New York. Catalogue by David Tathan.

1981 *Winslow Homer. The Charles Shipman Payson Gift to the Portland Museum of Art.* Coe Kerr Gallery, New York.

1983 *Winslow Homer in the 1880s. Watercolors, Drawings and Prints.* Everson Museum of Art, Syracuse, New York. Catalogue by David Tathan.

1983 *Winslow Homer. Watercolors.* Bowdoin College Museum of Art, Brunswick, Maine. Introduction by Philip C. Beam.

1984-1985 *Winslow Homer. The Croquet Game.* Yale University Art Gallery, New Haven, Connecticut; National Academy of Design, New York. Catalogue by David Park Curry.

1986 *Winslow Homer. Watercolors.* National Gallery of Art, Washington, D. C.; Amon Carter Museum, Fort Worth, Texas; Yale University Art Gallery, New Haven, Connecticut.

▷

Five Sketches of Young Boys, ca 1872
Black crayon on gray-blue paper
$10^{5}/_{8}$" × $18^{1}/_{8}$" (27 × 46.1 cm)
Cooper-Hewitt Museum
The Smithsonian Institution's National Museum of Design, New York

*We wish to thank the owners of the pictures reproduced herein, as well as those collectors
who did not want their name mentioned*

MUSEUMS

ANDOVER, MASSACHUSETTS
Addison Gallery of American Art

BOSTON
Museum of Fine Arts

BRUNSWICK, MAINE
Bowdoin College Museum of Art

BUFFALO, NEW YORK
Albright-Knox Art Gallery

LOS ANGELES
Los Angeles County Museum of Art

NEW BRITAIN, CONNECTICUT
New Britain Museum of
American Art

NEW HAVEN, CONNECTICUT
Yale University Art Gallery

NEW YORK
Brooklyn Museum
Cooper-Hewitt Museum
Metropolitan Museum of Art

PHILADELPHIA
Pennsylvania Academy of the
Fine Arts
Philadelphia Museum of Art

PITTSBURGH
Carnegie Institute

ROCHESTER
Memorial Art Gallery, University
of Rochester

SAINT LOUIS, MISSOURI
Art Museum

TOLEDO, OHIO
Museum of Art

WASHINGTON, D. C.
Library of Congress
National Gallery of Art
National Museum of American Art
Phillips Gallery

WATERVILLE, MAINE
Colby College Museum of Art

WILLIAMSTOWN,
MASSACHUSETTS
Sterling and Francine Clark Institute

PARIS
Palais de Tokyo

PRIVATE COLLECTION

The Thyssen Bornemisza Collection,
Lugano, Switzerland

PHOTOGRAPHS

Scott Hyde, New York
Joseph Szaszfai, New Haven
Mike Fisher, Washington, D. C.
E. Irving Blomstrann, New Britain
Eric Mitchell, Philadelphia
Otto Nelson, New York

LIST OF ILLUSTRATIONS

Abaco Island (On) 37
All in the Gay and Golden Weather 18
Army of the Potomac (The) 8
Artist's Studio in an Afternoon Fog (The) .. 67
At Sea — Signalling a Passing Steamer 50

Beach at Long Branch (The) 19
Berry Pickers (The) 20
Bivouac Fire on the Potomac (A) 30
Blown Away 35
Breezing Up 33

Cape Trinity, Saguenay River 90
Carnival (The) 31
Cotton Pickers (The) 28
Country School (The) 23
Croquet Match (The) 14
Croquet Players (The) 16
Cuban Hillside 81

Deer Drinking 60

Eight Bells 49
End of the Hunt (The) 61

Fallen Deer (The) 61
Fish and Butterflies 77
Fisherman in Quebec 87
Fog Warning 44
Fox Hunt 64

Gathering Autumn Leaves 26
Girl on a Swing 82
Girls on a Swing (Two) 83
Glass Windows 36
Gloucester Harbor 32
Good Pool (A) 63
Gulf Stream (The) 69

High Cliff 66
High Tide 39
Husking the Corn 12

Inside the Bar 34

Kissing the Moon 85

Life Boat (The) 73
Life-Line (The) 41
Life-Line (Drawing for The) 40
Long Branch, New Jersey 15

Morning Bell (The) 13

Northeaster 74

Our National Winter Exercise 10

Paddling at Dusk 58
Palm Trees 78
Parisian Ball (A) 11
Perils of the Sea 47
Prisoners from the Front 5

Right and Left 88
Robin's Note (The) 24
Rowing Home 59

Saved 41
Signal of Distress (The) 51
Sketches of Young Boys (Five) 95
Snap-The-Whip 21
St. John's River 79
Summer Night (A) 57
Sunlight and Shadow 25
Sunlight on the Coast 52

Three Days on the Front 9
Tree Roots on a Hillside 71
Trout Fishing 62
Turtle Pound (The) 80
Two Guides (The) 27

Undertow 42-43
Undertow (Study for) 54, 55

Wall, Nassau (A) 80
Waverly Oaks 17
West Point, Prout's Neck 75
Wreck (The) 72
Wounded Soldier 6

Young Girl 22
Young Soldier 7